ADA COMMUNITY LIBRARY
10664 W. VICTORY
BOISE, ID 83709

D0633083

Jefferson Davis

Confederate President

Colonial Leaders

Lord Baltimore
English Politician and Colonist

Benjamin Banneker
American Mathematician and Astronomer

Sir William Berkeley
Governor of Virginia

William Bradford
Governor of Plymouth Colony

Jonathan Edwards
Colonial Religious Leader

Benjamin Franklin
American Statesman, Scientist, and Writer

Anne Hutchinson
Religious Leader

Cotton Mather
Author, Clergyman, and Scholar

Increase Mather
Clergyman and Scholar

James Oglethorpe
Humanitarian and Soldier

William Penn
Founder of Democracy

Sir Walter Raleigh
English Explorer and Author

Caesar Rodney
American Patriot

John Smith
English Explorer and Colonist

Miles Standish
Plymouth Colony Leader

Peter Stuyvesant
Dutch Military Leader

George Whitefield
Clergyman and Scholar

Roger Williams
Founder of Rhode Island

John Winthrop
Politician and Statesman

John Peter Zenger
Free Press Advocate

Revolutionary War Leaders

John Adams
Second U.S. President

Ethan Allen
Revolutionary Hero

Benedict Arnold
Traitor to the Cause

King George III
English Monarch

Nathanael Greene
Military Leader

Nathan Hale
Revolutionary Hero

Alexander Hamilton
First U.S. Secretary of the Treasury

John Hancock
President of the Continental Congress

Patrick Henry
American Statesman and Speaker

John Jay
First Chief Justice of the Supreme Court

Thomas Jefferson
Author of the Declaration of Independence

John Paul Jones
Father of the U.S. Navy

Lafayette
French Freedom Fighter

James Madison
Father of the Constitution

Francis Marion
The Swamp Fox

James Monroe
American Statesman

Thomas Paine
Political Writer

Paul Revere
American Patriot

Betsy Ross
American Patriot

George Washington
First U.S. President

Famous Figures of the Civil War Era

Jefferson Davis
Confederate President

Frederick Douglass
Abolitionist and Author

Ulysses S. Grant
Military Leader and President

Stonewall Jackson
Confederate General

Robert E. Lee
Confederate General

Abraham Lincoln
Civil War President

William Sherman
Union General

Harriet Beecher Stowe
Author of Uncle Tom's Cabin

Sojourner Truth
Abolitionist, Suffragist, and Preacher

Harriet Tubman
Leader of the Underground Railroad

Famous Figures of the Civil War Era

Jefferson Davis

Confederate President

Joey Frazier

Arthur M. Schlesinger, jr.
Senior Consulting Editor

Chelsea House Publishers

Philadelphia

JB
DAVI

20.85

Produced by 21st Century Publishing and Communications, Inc.
New York, NY. http://www.21cpc.com

CHELSEA HOUSE PUBLISHERS
Production Manager Pamela Loos
Art Director Sara Davis
Director of Photography Judy L. Hasday
Managing Editor James D. Gallagher
Senior Production Editor J. Christopher Higgins

Staff for *JEFFERSON DAVIS*
Project Editor Anne Hill
Associate Art Director Takeshi Takahashi
Series Design Keith Trego

©2001 by Chelsea House Publishers, a subsidiary of Haights Cross
Communications. All rights reserved. Printed and bound in the
United States of America.

The Chelsea House World Wide Web address is
http://www.chelseahouse.com

First Printing
1 3 5 7 9 8 6 4 2

Library of Congress Cataloging-in-Publication Data

Frazier, Joey.
    Jefferson Davis / Joey Frazier.
        p.   cm. — (Famous figures of the Civil War era)
    Includes bibliographical references (p.   ) and index.
    ISBN 0-7910-6006-3 (HC) — ISBN 0-7910-6144-2 (PB)
        1. Davis, Jefferson, 1808–1889—Juvenile literature. 2. Presidents
—Confederate States of Amereica—Biography—Juvenile literature.
3. Statesmen—United States—Biography—Juvenile literature. [1. Davis,
Jefferson, 1808–1889. 2. Presidents —Confederate States of Amereica.]
I. Title. II. Series.

E467.1.D26 F68 2000
973.7'13'092—dc21   00-030339
[B]   CIP

Publisher's Note: In Colonial, Revolutionary War, and Civil War Era
America, there were no standard rules for spelling, punctuation,
capitalization, or grammar. Some of the quotations that appear in
the Colonial Leaders, Revolutionary War Leaders, and Famous
Figures of the Civil War Era series come from original documents
and letters written during this time in history. Original quotations
reflect writing inconsistencies of the period.

Contents

Jefferson Davis's first home also served as an inn (like this one pictured) for travelers to stop and rest. But he spent most of his early life on a large farm in Mississippi, where his father became a well-to-do cotton planter.

Early Life

In Christian County, Kentucky, just a few miles north of the border with Tennessee, the spring rains had stopped. The temperature was getting warmer every day, and summer was near. Samuel and Jane Davis were very excited because it was time for their baby to be born. Even though the Davises already had nine children—four boys and five girls—they somehow knew this baby would be special. Finally, the waiting was over, and on June 3, 1808, a baby boy came into the world. His parents named him Jefferson Finis Davis.

The Davis family lived in a four-room house

surrounded by 600 acres of land. Their home, which was larger than most other homes on the western **frontier,** even included glass windows. Most houses in Christian County were log cabins with only one or two rooms. Since the house was large, it also served as an inn where travelers often stayed. Samuel Davis called his inn The Wayfarers' Rest.

The Davis family enjoyed a comfortable life. Jefferson's father, who had been a soldier and officer in the American Revolution, was a very respected man. But Samuel Davis's military days were over. Now, he raised **thoroughbred** horses on the family's farm.

In February 1809, only eight months after Jefferson Davis was born, another special baby boy came into the world. He was born in a one-room log cabin less than 100 miles from the Davis farm. His name was Abraham Lincoln. Because the Lincoln family was poor, young Abe had to work very hard to get an education. Without the opportunity to attend good schools, Lincoln had to use his hands as well as his mind to improve himself before serving the people as the 16th president of the United States.

While he was a successful man, Samuel Davis wanted to do more than run an inn and raise horses. At that time, many people in the South were making a lot of money growing cotton. Samuel decided that he too could prosper by starting a cotton **plantation**, and in 1811, the family moved to the Louisiana Territory. The next year, they moved again to the Mississippi Territory near the town of Woodville. At the age of 56, Samuel settled in Mississippi, which was not yet a state, and became a cotton planter. The Davises named their new home Rosemont.

Like most boys during that time, young Jefferson liked to hunt, and he spent much of his time outdoors. But schooling was important for the boy, and at the age of five he began attending class in a log cabin nearby. Every day Jefferson walked to school with his sister Mary, who was seven years old.

But Samuel was not happy with Jefferson's progress at the local school, and he decided the boy would get a better education at another school.

Jefferson's father chose Saint Thomas Aquinas School in Kentucky, a highly respected Catholic school run by monks of the Dominican order.

Kentucky was a long way from Mississippi, and the journey would take several weeks. There were no steamboats on the Mississippi River and no railroads across the countryside to make traveling faster or easier. The only way to Kentucky was on horseback or on foot.

Since Jefferson was too young to make the journey alone, his father had to find someone to go with him. As it happened, Major Thomas Hinds, a soldier who had fought in the War of 1812 against Britain along with Jefferson's older brother Joseph, was going to Kentucky at just the right time. The boy could go along with Major Hinds.

The trip could be quite dangerous because Jefferson and the major traveled through Indian country. As more and more settlers moved into Indian lands in Kentucky, the Indians and set- tlers were often at war. But young Jefferson was

Growing up in the South, young Jefferson was familiar with scenes like this—black slaves picking cotton in the fields of large plantations.

not afraid. He was already a very brave boy who looked forward to this adventure.

Jefferson and Major Hinds had to live off the land, hunting and fishing for their food. At night they slept outdoors on the ground. When they arrived in Nashville, Tennessee, they stopped for a visit with a famous general, Andrew Jackson. Spending a few weeks at General Jackson's home, the Hermitage, was great fun for Jefferson. He knew General Jackson was a great hero because he had defeated the British at the Battle of New Orleans during the War of 1812. Several years later, Andrew Jackson would become the seventh president of the United States.

Finally, Jefferson and Hinds arrived at Saint Thomas Aquinas School, where Jefferson met Father Wilson, the school's head. Jefferson was so impressed with the kindness of the Catholic monks that he even thought about becoming a Catholic. One day, he asked Father Wilson if he could **convert** to the Catholic religion. Being a very wise man, Father Wilson knew Jefferson was still too young to make such an important decision. He told the boy it would be better to wait until he was older.

Jefferson was eager to be accepted by the other

boys at school, which sometimes got him into trouble. One time the older boys asked Jefferson to blow out the candle that burned in their room as a night light. Not knowing what the boys had in mind, Jefferson did what they asked.

As soon as the light went out, the older boys began throwing food at one another. Hearing the commotion, Father Wilson rushed to the room and stumbled into the darkness. Finally, he found the candle. When he lit it, standing there in the orange glow was Jefferson. The boy appeared to be the only one awake, and Father Wilson asked Jefferson for an explanation.

Even though he was in a lot of trouble, Jefferson did not tell on his friends. He only said that he was the one who had blown out the candle. After a long talk with Father Wilson, Jefferson went to his room in tears. He never got into trouble at school again.

After attending Saint Thomas Aquinas for three years, 11-year-old Jefferson returned home in Mississippi to visit his family. They were glad to see him, and he was happy to be home where he could hunt and enjoy the outdoors again. But Samuel Davis still felt his son was someone very special, and he wanted Jefferson to continue his education.

There was a school closer to the Davis home— the Wilkinson Academy. It was a good school, but the principal was very strict. After attending the academy for a little while, Jefferson decided he did not like the **discipline**. Going to his father, he asked if he could leave the school. Samuel Davis said yes, but with one condition— Jefferson had to decide if he wanted to work with his mind or with his hands.

Anxious to get out of school, the boy replied that he would work with his hands. He soon found out just how hard that kind of work can be. His father sent him to pick cotton in the fields, one of the hardest jobs on a plantation. Not only was it extremely hot in the fields, but picking cotton hurt his fingers, often causing them to bleed. Jefferson soon decided it was better to work with his mind, and he happily returned to school.

Continuing his education, the teenager went off to Transylvania College in Lexington, Kentucky, when he was 15. His schoolwork included studying Greek and Latin, and he loved to read all the books he could find. Still, the school was far from home, and Jefferson missed his family. He especially missed his father, who passed away while he was at school.

Despite the death of his father, Jefferson continued his education. In 1824, his brother Joseph arranged for the 16-year-old to attend the United States Military Academy at West Point. Founded in 1802 and located along the Hudson River in New York State, West Point trains young men to be army officers.

Jefferson did not want to be in the army, but he knew studying at West Point was an important step in completing his education. At the school, he became friends with other students, including young men like Robert E. Lee of Virginia, who would play important roles in Jefferson's later life.

At West Point, Jefferson learned to become an officer in the U.S. army, where he would lead and train soldiers as this officer is doing.

While the young man was not a top student at West Point, he proved to be courageous. One day, he and his classmates were learning about fireballs, which are small bombs much like

modern-day hand grenades. When one acciden-
tally became ignited, Jefferson was the first to
react. The teacher shouted, "Run for your lives!"
and fled. Moving in a flash, Jefferson grabbed the
bomb and threw it out a window. His quick
thinking and bravery saved the lives of many of
his classmates.

At West Point, Jefferson also learned to be a
good soldier and gained a sense of honor, duty,
and responsibility. Although he probably did
not realize it until many years later, the most
important lesson he learned at West Point was
that "only trained soldiers win wars."

Jefferson's early service as a soldier included keeping peace between Native Americans and white settlers who were moving west. Indian warriors fought fiercely to keep their land.

Soldier, Planter, Politician

When Jefferson graduated from West Point in July 1828, he held the rank of second lieutenant in the United States army. Before taking his first assignment, he visited his family and spent some time at his brother Joseph's cotton plantation, The Hurricane. Finally it was time to report for duty at the Jefferson Barracks in St. Louis, Missouri.

Jefferson took his servant, black **slave** James Pemberton, with him. Although James was considered the property of the young soldier, he and Jefferson were close friends. Over the years, James traveled everywhere with Jefferson and took good care of him.

After a short stay in St. Louis, Jefferson was transferred to Fort Crawford in what is now the state of Wisconsin. Back then, the area was called the Michigan Territory. Fort Crawford was on the frontier, and many Native American tribes and white settlers lived there.

Relations between the tribes and the settlers were not always friendly. Many Indians were angry because settlers were taking over their lands and building homes and towns in their territories.

One day, Jefferson had a close call with a band of Native Americans. The fort needed some sturdy logs for repairs, and Jefferson was moving upriver on a raft searching for trees. Suddenly a group of Indian warriors in canoes appeared on the river and began paddling after Jefferson and his men. The raft was slow, and Jefferson had to think fast to save his men from being attacked. Looking around, he grabbed up a large blanket and rigged a sail for the raft. With the sail taking the wind, Jefferson and his men outran the Indians. His quick thinking saved everyone's life.

As an army officer, Jefferson was often on the move, going from one post to another. From 1829 to 1831, he was stationed at Fort Winnebago in the northern part of the Michigan Territory. There, he had many opportunities to meet and observe Native Americans in the area. While at Winnebago, Jefferson caught pneumonia during a cold, wet winter and almost died. Thanks to the good care of James Pemberton, the young officer recovered.

In 1831, Jefferson was again ordered to another post, this time in Dubuque, in what is now the state of Iowa. **Squatters** from the East were settling on Indian lands, and the Indians were becoming angry and resentful. Earlier, the United States had sent soldiers to force the squatters out, but they refused to move. At the same time, the U.S. government was forcing

ADA COMMUNITY LIBRARY

many Indian tribes to give up their land and move west of the Mississippi River.

Jefferson was good at gaining people's trust and getting them to listen to his opinions. His commander asked him to try and settle the conflict between the Indians and the settlers. It was Jefferson's job to talk the settlers into leaving Indian lands until a treaty could be worked out.

But the tension along the frontier continued. One Indian tribe called the Sac and Fox, under their leader, Black Hawk, resisted being removed from their land. In 1832, when a group of settlers attacked Black Hawk's village, the conflict turned into war. Hundreds of men from the territory formed a **militia** to fight the Indians until regular army troops could be gathered.

The Black Hawk War did not last long. More than 1,000 militiamen and soldiers fought three battles with Black Hawk's warriors and finally crushed the Indian resistance. They also cruelly killed innocent Indian women and children. Although Jefferson served in the war, he did not

Although it was Jefferson's duty to fight Black Hawk (at left, with his son), he greatly admired and respected the brave warrior.

approve of the actions of the militia. He believed that even his enemies should be treated with honor and dignity. When Black Hawk was captured and placed under Jefferson Davis's command, Jefferson showed him respect because the

Indian leader was a great warrior.

Following the war, Jefferson moved to yet another post. This time he went back to Fort Crawford. His job there was to **recruit** young men into the U.S. army. Since Jefferson was good at talking to people and persuading them, he was successful.

While Jefferson was at Fort Crawford, he fell in love with Sarah Knox Taylor and decided he wanted to marry her. Sarah was the daughter of his commander, Colonel Zachary Taylor. (Colonel Taylor later became a famous general and the 12th president of the United States.)

But Colonel Taylor did not approve of young Jefferson as a husband for his daughter. He did not want Sarah to marry a soldier. Even if Jefferson and Sarah thought of going against her father's wishes, they didn't get the chance. Suddenly Jefferson was transferred once again, this time to a rugged part of the frontier in western Arkansas.

Jefferson missed Sarah very much, and he had to make a decision about what to do. In 1835 he resigned from the army and moved to Kentucky, where Sarah had gone to live with an aunt. The young couple were married in her aunt's house and almost immediately moved south into Jefferson's home state of Mississippi.

Jefferson had decided that he wanted to be a cotton planter, but he had no land. His brother Joseph came to his aid and gave Jefferson and Sarah some land about 15 miles south of Vicksburg, a town on the Mississippi River. From now on, Jefferson Davis would be a cotton planter.

Starting a plantation was hard work, but with the help of James Pemberton, Jefferson began preparing the land for planting. Trees had to be cut and brush had to be cleared

Southern cotton planters were successful largely because of Eli Whitney, who invented the first cotton gin in 1793. The machine used teeth attached to a rotating cylinder to pull cotton fibers through a comblike structure. The large cotton seeds could not pass through the comb. This method of easily separating the cotton fibers from the seeds greatly increased cotton production in the South. As cotton production expanded, slavery also grew because more people were needed to work in the fields planting and picking the cotton.

away. Because the fields were filled with so many prickly bushes called briars, Jefferson named his plantation Briarfield.

Jefferson was just getting Briarfield established when he and Sarah decided to visit Bayou Sara in Louisiana, near Sarah's sister. An outbreak of malaria, a disease that often occurred in the heat and humidity of southern summers, had occured near Briarfield. Spread by the bite of mosquitoes, malaria germs enter a person's bloodstream, causing high fever and chills. There were no medicines to prevent malaria, and the disease took the lives of many people in those days.

Jefferson thought he and Sarah would be safe farther north in Louisiana, but it was too late. They both came down with malaria and suffered the chills and fever. Jefferson finally recovered, but Sarah did not. In September 1835, only three months after their marriage, Sarah died.

Jefferson was heartbroken. For a long time, he did not want to see or talk to anybody. He left Mississippi and began moving from place to place. For a while, he and James lived in Havana, Cuba, and then traveled to New York City. Later, he visited an old friend from Transylvania College who lived in Washington, D.C.

When Jefferson and James finally moved back to Mississippi, Jefferson still could not forget Sarah. He seemed uninterested in doing anything but reading his many books. While James managed Briarfield, Jefferson shut himself up in his house, seeing no one.

But Jefferson was only in his 30s, and he could not hide away for the rest of his life. Around that time, he found that he was interested in politics, so he decided to run as a representative to the Mississippi state **legislature** in 1843. Although he did not win, he had ended his isolation from the world. He did not know it then, but this was the beginning of his public life.

By this time, Jefferson had become a successful cotton planter, but he still lived alone. Then he met a 17-year-old woman, who was the daughter of a close friend. Her name was Varina Howell.

Jefferson's second wife, Varina Howell, was never far from his side as he pursued his careers as soldier, planter, and politician.

She was visiting Jefferson's brother Joseph for a Christmas holiday when she and Jefferson met and fell in love.

In 1844, the young couple became engaged, and they were married the following year. In that same year Jefferson won his first public office when he was elected to the House of Representatives. Many leaders in Congress were impressed with Jefferson's knowledge and his ability to make people listen to his ideas.

Jefferson had only been in office for about a year when the United States and Mexico went to war. The conflict involved a dispute with Mexico about where the border between Texas and Mexico should be. The United States claimed that the border was the Rio Grande River, while Mexico said it was farther north along the Nueces River.

Jefferson felt it was his duty to volunteer to fight since he was already a trained soldier. He resigned from Congress in 1846 to accept an appointment as colonel of the Mississippi Rifles. Moving with his regiment to the Rio Grande, Jefferson came under the command of his former father-in-law, General Zachary Taylor.

Most of the battles of the Mexican-American War were fought in Mexico. Jefferson and his troops entered Mexico, moving south toward the capital, Mexico City. At a place called Buena Vista, about 300 miles north of Mexico City, Jefferson led his troops into battle. Even though he was hit by a bullet that shattered his heel, he stayed in his saddle for another eight hours commanding his men.

On that day in February 1847, Jefferson helped save the United States Army from defeat. Although he was wounded and outnumbered, he ordered his men into a "V" formation, keeping the Mexican soldiers from getting behind American lines. Because of Jefferson's quick thinking, the Americans won the battle, and he became known as the hero of Buena Vista.

When the war ended the next year, Jefferson was warmly received at home. Seeing how popular he was, the governor of Mississippi appointed Jefferson to the United States Senate to finish the term of a senator who had recently died. Once again,

**As a U.S. senator, Jefferson lived in Washington, D.C.
His skills as a speaker and leader in the Senate made
him an outstanding member of his political party.**

Jefferson and Varina returned to Washington, D.C.

Jefferson belonged to the Democratic Party,
whose members in the South believed strongly
in states' rights. Those who championed states'

rights believed that the U.S. Constitution allowed each state to govern itself without too much interference from the central government in Washington. They also supported slavery. Both of these issues caused great arguments and conflict between Southerners and Northerners. Most people in the North strongly opposed states' rights and slavery.

Jefferson was a firm believer in states' rights and he did not oppose slavery. As a senator, his abilities as a speaker made him a leader among the Democrats. But he was thinking about a higher office. In 1851, he resigned from the senate to run for governor of Mississippi. Perhaps because he had been ill and because his opponent reportedly ran an underhanded campaign, Jefferson lost the election.

But Jefferson did not stay out of public life for very long. In 1852, he accepted an appointment to serve as secretary of war to President Franklin Pierce. Most of Jefferson's duties involved working with the U.S. army to strengthen its fighting power, and he did an excellent job. Under Jefferson's leadership, the army grew larger and stronger. He also improved living conditions for soldiers and raised their pay. Jefferson's term of office was over in 1857, and he returned to his seat in the Senate.

By this time, however, tension between the North and the South over states' rights and slavery had become intense. Some Southerners were talking about separating from the United States. They wanted to **secede** and become an independent nation with their own government. Although Jefferson maintained his strong support for the South, he worked very hard to keep the Southern and Northern states together.

Everyone was divided over the issue of slavery. Many Northerners were **abolitionists,** who were determined to see that slavery was done away with. Most Southerners were just as determined to keep slavery in place. Most of the South was a region of farms and plantations, and slave owners argued that they needed slave labor to work their fields. They also said that slavery was a tradition in the South and that it was not illegal under the Constitution.

The agricultural society of the South was built on slave labor, which many people in the North opposed. One person who hated slavery was writer Harriet Beecher Stowe. She gained a tremendous amount of attention when she wrote the novel *Uncle Tom's Cabin*, which described the torture and abuse of slaves. The novel was extremely popular in the North, but many Southerners hated it. Some people believe Harriet Beecher Stowe's book helped start the Civil War.

The North was primarily a region of industry, and workers in the factories and mines were free. It seemed that the North and the South could never reach an agreement.

Then in 1860, Abraham Lincoln was elected president. Lincoln was a member of the Republican Party, which opposed slavery, and he was extremely unpopular in the South. Many Southerners feared that Lincoln would work to abolish slavery. They believed that the national government did not want to listen to their problems.

The state of South Carolina especially resented

the North and the national government. The people feared that their cotton trade would be ruined if slavery was abolished. In December 1860, leaders of South Carolina declared the state was going to secede from the United States. By February 1, 1861, six other states, including Mississippi, had joined South Carolina. On hearing that his state had left the **Union**, Jefferson gave his final speech as a United States senator and resigned his office. He was ready to take his place with the people of Mississippi.

Southerners gathered as Jefferson was inaugurated president of a new nation. As the leader of the Confederacy, he worked hard to keep up Southern hopes for victory and independence.

3

President of a New Nation

Jefferson was 52 years old when he left Washington, D.C., and he had been ill. Thinking that he would be called on to command Southern troops if war broke out, he wanted time to get well. But leaders from the Southern states, who met in Montgomery, Alabama, in February 1861, had other ideas for him. Jefferson was a military hero and had been a well-respected senator. These men felt he would be the right person to lead a new nation, the **Confederate States of America**.

Jefferson was resting in his rose garden at Briarfield when he saw a horse and rider gallop up the road.

Jumping from his horse, the man handed Jefferson a message that would make him forever famous. Southerners had elected Jefferson Davis temporary president of the Confederate States of America.

Jefferson was reluctant to take the office, but he felt it was his duty to serve the people of the South he loved so much. He hoped he would only have to be president for a short time until a permanent government could be established. Jefferson really wanted to return to military service, but he accepted the position. For now, he had a important job to do in leading the Confederacy.

It was a cold February day when Jefferson stepped into a small boat at Briarfield landing, wondering where his journey would take him. His slaves rowed him out of the shallow waters of the landing and three miles down the Mississippi to the large steamboat that carried the new president to Vicksburg.

Once in the city, he was greeted by marching bands and parading soldiers. From there, Jefferson boarded a train that took him to Montgomery,

Alabama, the capital of the Confederacy. On February 18, 1861, Jefferson Davis was **inaugurated** as president of the Confederate States of America.

Tired from his long trip and worried that war might soon come, Jefferson still knew he had to give hope to the people of the South. He delivered a powerful speech, giving Southerners hope and courage for the journey that lay ahead. The South and the North were headed for a long and bloody **civil war**.

Jefferson's first task in Montgomery was to set up the new government. He needed to appoint members to his cabinet, the group of men who would help him make decisions. He tried to appoint at least one person from each state in the Confederacy, but this proved difficult. Some very ambitious men wanted powerful jobs, but they were not good leaders. Others complained about the jobs they were offered. Jefferson had many friends, but he also had many enemies, even within the new government.

Jefferson tried to work out a peace **treaty** with

the United States, hoping to avoid a war that he knew would be difficult for the Confederacy. The South did not have the factories to make the weapons and machines needed for war. There was no trained army, and few railroads to transport soldiers and supplies. But the South did have several excellent military officers, including some who had trained at West Point. Others, like Robert E. Lee, had also served in the Mexican War.

But a treaty was not possible. President Lincoln did not recognize the Confederacy as a new nation. The Southern states, he declared, were in rebellion against the United States, and their actions were unconstitutional. Confederate leaders declared they had a constitutional right to leave the union of states if it trampled on the states' rights. Each side believed completely in its cause and each accused the other of **aggression**.

Finally, the arguments ended at the United States military base called Fort Sumter in the harbor of Charleston, South Carolina. Both the North and the South would need the fort

Both North and South recruited troops when the South seceded. Here, Union troops board trains that will carry them off to war.

if war came, and many Southerners wanted to fight to take it. Jefferson wanted to find a peaceful solution, but he also had to boost the morale of his people.

The problem was resolved for Jefferson when South Carolina demanded that Union forces leave

The first shots of the Civil War were fired at Fort Sumter in Charleston Harbor in South Carolina. The South needed to control Fort Sumter so it could use the port for trade and transportation. Union major Robert Anderson, who commanded U.S. troops at the fort, had once been a friend of Jefferson Davis. Although Jefferson did not want to harm his friend, he ordered General P.G.T. Beauregard to take the fort. Beauregard shelled Fort Sumter for 34 hours before Anderson raised the white flag of surrender. Amazingly, no one on either side was killed in the opening battle of the Civil War.

Fort Sumter. When President Lincoln refused, Southern forces in Charleston fired on Fort Sumter on April 12, 1861. The shelling began at 4:30 A.M. and continued throughout the morning and into the afternoon. Around 2 P.M., Jefferson received a message that Union forces had surrendered. The South could celebrate its first victory of the four-year Civil War that was to follow.

After the first shots of the war were fired, more Southern states, including Virginia, joined the Confederacy. Because Virginia was a very important and powerful state, the new Confederate Congress voted to make its largest city, Richmond, the new Confederate

Guns at Fort Sumter return the Confederate fire as the Civil War begins. The final surrender of the fort was the first victory for the Confederacy.

capital. Richmond was also fairly close to Washington, D.C., and could serve as a symbol of the South's determination to carry on the fight.

Jefferson and his family moved to Richmond, where he was now close to the North's military lines around Washington. The president did not have long to wait before the two sides clashed.

In July 1861, North and South met near the town of Manassas Junction, about 30 miles north of Richmond. Manassas was important to the Confederacy. A railroad line that could transport troops and supplies across Virginia's western mountains ran through the town. Union forces were preparing to attack, and Confederate troops had to stop them.

At a large creek called Bull Run, Confederate troops under generals P.G.T. Beauregard and Joseph Johnston lined up on the southern side, ready to defend their position. Knowing a battle was coming, Jefferson wanted to be part of it. When he received a message from General Beauregard that there had been a **skirmish**, he hurried by train to Manassas Junction.

But Jefferson did not get there in time for the big battle that occurred on July 21, 1861. When he finally arrived, he could see the black smoke from the muskets and hear the roar of cannon fire, but the battle was nearly over. Confederate soldiers had overwhelmed Union troops, who retreated to the outskirts of Washington.

After the victory, Jefferson wanted his generals to pursue the Union army. But the soldiers were tired and hungry and needed rest. So the generals waited. Still, Jefferson and the entire South were more confident after winning the battle at Bull Run.

Although the Confederacy celebrated its victory, it had come at a high price. Many soldiers from both sides died on the battlefield, among them Jefferson's nephew, Edward Anderson. The saddened president found the young man in a hospital tent after the fighting was over. Edward's death made Jefferson realize that the war would be hard and costly.

As much as Jefferson wanted to be a part of the fighting, he had a lot of work to do in Richmond. He returned to the capital to order supplies for the army and arrange for reinforcements to help Confederate soldiers hold their positions. He also met with his advisers and generals to discuss the **strategies** for carrying on the war.

While the battle at Manassas was over, other

Jefferson (seated, fourth from left) discusses war strategies with his cabinet. Disagreements with his advisers often put great pressure on Jefferson.

battles were brewing in the Confederate government. Jefferson was fighting his own war of words with General Beauregard and General Johnston. Since Jefferson had been trained in the military, he felt he was capable of telling his generals how to run the war. They often disagreed. Sometimes the generals argued amongst themselves about who had the highest rank in the army.

Many of Jefferson's advisers also complained about his decisions. During 1862, three different secretaries of war served in his cabinet. Although Jefferson recognized that his ideas often clashed with those of his advisers and generals, he was disappointed that they were at odds with him.

As the fighting went on, Jefferson, who was ill much of the time, was under a lot of pressure. He struggled to give hope to Southerners and to keep the war effort alive, but the conflicts within the government wounded the Confederacy. Still, in spite of the problems, in 1862, Jefferson was elected permanent president of the Confederate States of America.

As the war went on, Jefferson (third from left) often visited battlefields. Here, with General Thomas "Stonewall" Jackson at his right, he talks with General Robert E. Lee, who points to the battle raging below.

The War
Rages On

Even though the Confederacy was only one year old, it had won the first battles of the Civil War. But disagreements within his government and later battlefield defeats were taking a heavy toll on Jefferson. In February 1862, his army was outnumbered and short of food and other supplies. His policies were becoming unpopular. Some said he was making too many decisions by himself. Others thought he was not taking enough risks to win the war. Jefferson did not believe in taking risks unless they were absolutely necessary. He thought the South should defend itself against the North but not attack. He hoped that if the South held on long enough, the North would get tired of the conflict.

To add to Jefferson's struggles as the Confederate president, he suffered a personal loss in 1862. His good friend from West Point, General Albert Sidney Johnston, died in the Battle of Shiloh, fought in the west in Tennessee. Although shot in the leg, Johnston had stayed with his troops to lead the fighting. But the wound was serious, and the general bled to death before the battle was over.

The Battle of Shiloh was one of the bloodiest of the Civil War. Nearly 24,000 soldiers were killed, wounded, or missing. It was also a major defeat for the South. In winning the battle, the Union forces had begun taking control of the western part of the Confederacy.

Soon after their victory at Shiloh, Union forces won more battles in Tennessee. Then, the Union navy captured the city of New Orleans and sailed up the Mississippi River. Arkansas, Louisiana, and Texas were now cut off from the rest of the

Confederacy. In the East, a Union army was also advancing into Virginia and heading toward Richmond. To keep his family safe, Jefferson sent Varina and their children to the city of Raleigh, North Carolina. Left alone, it was another sad time for Jefferson, who missed the comfort of his family.

By April 1862, Union forces were only four miles from Richmond, which was defended by General Joseph Johnston's army. Jefferson and General Robert E. Lee had hurried directly from Richmond to observe the battle, during which Johnston was wounded. Seeing that General Johnston was hurt, Jefferson made a quick and important decision. He appointed Lee commander of the entire Army of Northern Virginia and placed him in charge of the area outside Richmond.

Many people thought Jefferson had made a bad decision because each leader had different ideas about how to win the war. Jefferson wanted to send more Confederate armies to fight the Union in the West. Lee thought the best strategy

General Robert Edward Lee became a hero during the Civil War for his compassionate character and amazing knowledge of battle strategy. Lee understood how to use trenches called earthworks to keep an attacking army from advancing, and he led Confederate soldiers to many victories. But he also suffered a terrible defeat at the Battle of Gettysburg in Pennsylvania. Lee's defeat, which he declared was his fault and not that of his officers or soldiers, is often called the turning point of the Civil War.

was to drive out Northern armies in Virginia and even **invade** the North. At the same time, General Thomas "Stonewall" Jackson was successful in fighting off Union troops in the mountains of Virginia.

As it turned out, Jefferson made a very wise decision in appointing Robert E. Lee. Unlike Jefferson's other generals, Lee got along well with the president, even if they did not always agree. Lee began his campaign by driving the Northern army away from Richmond and also won two important victories in battles in Maryland and Virginia.

In late 1862, Jefferson did not realize how close he was to winning the war. People in the North were tired of the fighting. It also seemed as if Union generals were not aggressive enough in taking their armies into Virginia, the heartland of the Confederacy. Many in the North wanted to work out a peace treaty with the Confederacy.

President Lincoln knew he had to do something to build hope and confidence in the North. In January 1863, he issued an important document, the **Emancipation Proclamation**. The proclamation freed all the slaves in the Southern states that were fighting the Union. After the proclamation, Northern states began recruiting free African Americans into the Union army. Before that, blacks were not allowed to serve.

Southerners were angered by both Lincoln's proclamation and the idea of African Americans fighting against them. While the Confederates determined to fight even harder, Southerners were suffering from food shortages, and prices were very high. Jefferson had tried to get help from Europe, but England and other nations did not want to get involved.

President Abraham Lincoln will always be remembered for having issued the Emancipation Proclamation, which freed all the slaves in the Southern states.

The Confederacy was also losing in the West. The city of Vicksburg, in Jefferson's home state, was under **siege** from a Union army. Jefferson desperately wanted to send an army to Mississippi, but Lee convinced him to make a bold move and invade the North. Lee's strategy was to lead his army into northern Pennsylvania, which would threaten Washington, D.C. Although Jefferson believed the plan was too risky, he and his cabinet approved it. General Lee had earned the respect of Jefferson and the Southern armies.

In early July, Lee met the Union army at Gettysburg, Pennsylvania. For three blistering hot days, the two armies fought back and forth. Losses were terrible as soldiers on both sides fought fiercely. In the end, the Confederates could not overcome Union forces, and Lee was forced to retreat to Virginia. Only a day after the battle, the city of Vicksburg fell to Union troops. Other Union forces took the key city of Chattanooga, Tennessee, and the way was open for a Union army to march to Atlanta, Georgia. The war in the West was lost.

By the beginning of 1864, Jefferson was losing the confidence of the Southern people. Confederate armies were losing battles, and food, clothing, and weapons were in short supply. The Confederacy was nearly **bankrupt**, and many were urging General Lee to replace Jefferson as the leader of the Confederacy. Lee always refused, declaring that he had confidence in President Davis.

In the fall of 1864, the Confederacy seemed doomed to defeat. A Union army had taken the city of Atlanta and was marching through Georgia, destroying railroads and farms and plantations. Desperate to bring the conflict to an end, Jefferson sent a group of men to President Lincoln to try to make peace. Lincoln offered $400 million to plantation owners for the slaves that would be freed, but he refused to recognize the Confederacy as an independent nation. The Southern people, Lincoln said, were resisting the laws of the United States. Jefferson could not accept such terms. The war went on, but the end was near.

In the spring of 1865, 56-year-old Jefferson once again became ill, but he continued his busy schedule and tried to stay in good spirits. Then he suffered a tragic blow when his young son Joseph accidently fell from a porch at the family home in Richmond and died. Jefferson suffered further distress when he had to send his family to safety in North Carolina. A Union army had invaded Virginia and approached Richmond.

The bad news came on a Sunday in April when Jefferson was attending a church service. General Lee sent the message that Union forces had broken through the Confederate lines, and the general could not hold Richmond. Jefferson and his cabinet had to leave the city at once. He planned to move the government to Danville, Virginia, but Union soldiers were searching the countryside, trying to find him.

In one of his last acts as president of the Confederacy, Jefferson ordered his troops to set fire to Richmond and leave the city. But by the time he had issued the order, Union soldiers were already in Richmond, and much of the city was burned. After Richmond fell into

Union hands, a tall man wearing a black coat and stovepipe hat was seen walking through the streets. President Abraham Lincoln was inspecting the damage to the city, even looking in Jefferson's house.

With the fall of Richmond, the war came to its close. Lee's army was surrounded, and he had no choice but to give up. On April 9, 1865, General Lee surrendered his army to Union General Ulysses S. Grant at Appomattox Courthouse in Virginia. Jefferson cried when he heard the news, but he still refused to admit defeat. He believed he could lead the Confederacy once again if his soldiers could keep on fighting along the Mississippi in the West. It was not a realistic hope. Shortly after Lee's surrender, other Confederate armies began surrendering to Union forces.

Once Jefferson left Richmond, he and what was left of his cabinet wandered from town to town, trying to avoid capture by Union soldiers. Then, in the middle of April, Jefferson heard the news that President Abraham Lincoln had been

Richmond burns out of control as its citizens flee the city. Leaving Richmond, Jefferson still hoped that he could lead Confederate troops to fight in the West.

shot and killed as he watched a play in Washington, D.C. Although they had been enemies, Jefferson was upset that the leader of the United States had been so cruelly murdered.

At the news that the South had surrendered, these Confederate soldiers sadly rolled up their beloved battle flag for the last time.

Some in the North claimed that Jefferson had ordered the attack on President Lincoln. The accusation angered Jefferson. He had always been an honorable man, even in the midst of the war. Many Northerners believed the rumors, including Andrew Johnson, who had been the vice president under Lincoln. After Lincoln's death, Johnson became the new president of the United States. He declared that Jefferson was an outlaw and should be hanged.

Avoiding Union soldiers, Jefferson made his way south and caught up with his family at Irwinville, Georgia. They had no house but slept in a tent outdoors and were protected only by a few Confederate soldiers. Early in the morning of May 10, 1865, Union troops surrounded Jefferson and his family. With the capture of the president of the Confederacy, the war was truly over.

For Jefferson, life after the war began with his imprisonment in a Union jail. When he was freed, he returned to the South as a hero. Finally settling in New Orleans, Louisiana, he lectured and wrote about his experiences as a Southern leader.

Life After the War

After his capture, officials moved Jefferson from one southern city to another, finally putting him in prison at Fort Monroe, Virginia. Now Jefferson was in the same place where the Indian warrior Black Hawk had been a prisoner. Jefferson was without family or friends, and many Southerners felt no sympathy for him. They blamed him for losing the war.

The former president of the Confederacy remained in prison for two years. His cell had one small window. Two guards marched outside his cell at all times, and he had no privacy. A ditch filled with water surrounded the prison, making it difficult to escape.

The official in charge, General Nelson Miles, hated Jefferson, and treated him like a criminal. He was not allowed any visitors and he had no books except the Bible. At night, lighted lanterns kept his cell so bright that he could barely sleep. Because Jefferson's guards would not give him a fork or spoon, he had to eat his meals with his fingers.

One of Miles's worst acts was to order iron bands with chains called shackles to be placed around Jefferson's ankles. The shackles made it difficult for Jefferson to walk and also rubbed against his ankles, causing them to bleed. When some newspapers learned of Miles's treatment of Jefferson, they wrote that the shackles were too cruel a punishment. Miles finally ordered the shackles to be removed.

As Jefferson suffered in prison, President Johnson was trying to decide what to do about the former Confederate president. Johnson realized it would be hard to convict Jefferson in a court of law, and he tried to get Jefferson to apply for a pardon. But Jefferson refused. Asking for a pardon says that a person did something wrong but can be forgiven. Jefferson declared he needed no pardon because he had broken no laws. He merely led a new nation that tried to legally separate from the United States. Only a court could decide the matter, and Jefferson was confident he could win. Still, officials did not schedule a trial.

Finally, in 1866, Varina started a campaign to free her husband. Many people in the North now agreed that Jefferson should be released. He was even becoming popular in the South once more. Many Northerners and Southerners felt that Jefferson had suffered long enough. With the help of a lawyer from New York, Jefferson was finally released from prison and all charges against him were dropped. He never had a chance to prove his innocence at a trial.

Jefferson returned to Richmond, where a large crowd greeted him warmly. His bravery and endurance made him a hero once more to the people of the South he loved so much. But at the time, he did not want to stay in the South or the North. Although free to move wherever he wanted, he had lost the right to be a citizen of the United States.

After spending some time in Canada, Jefferson decided he could not endure the cold climate. With his family, he moved first to the island of Cuba and then to New Orleans. The people of New Orleans also gave him a hero's welcome. But Louisiana was not Mississippi, and Jefferson longed for his Briarfield home.

Returning to Briarfield, Jefferson found his plantation in ruins. During the war, Union forces had burned the house, and the fields were overgrown with weeds. Jefferson and his family could not stay there, and his doctor recommended a trip to Europe. He needed to be far from the hurtful memories of his past struggles. After a stay in England and France, Jefferson was rested enough to return home. But he did not go back to Briarfield.

Jefferson and Varina moved to Memphis,

Jefferson did not retire to a quiet private life in his later years. He lectured and wrote up until his death in 1889.

Tennessee, where Jefferson took a job as head of an insurance company. The company went out of business in 1874. That same year, Jefferson's brother Joseph died. Soon after, his young son William also died.

Jefferson, 62 at the time, was devastated and mentally exhausted. Of his seven children, only his daughter, Winnie Anne, remained alive. Despite his losses, he tried to rebuild Briarfield. But he was getting too old to run a plantation.

After another trip to Europe to help recover his health, Jefferson returned to Memphis and began working for the Mississippi Valley Association, a company formed to help people from Europe who wanted to move to Mississippi. Again he had bad luck. The company folded after two years. At the age of 70, Jefferson seemed to have no place to go and no work.

Although his health was better, Jefferson was too old for a regular job. He was pleased, however, when Mississippi asked him to represent the state in the U.S. Senate. But he had to refuse. Because he would never again be a U.S. citizen, he could not serve. Instead, he retired to a new home, called Beauvoir, near New Orleans, and began to write a history of the Confederacy. After three years, he finished the book, titled *The Rise and Fall of the Confederate Government.*

Because his family needed the money, at the

age of 78, Jefferson began a lecture tour through the South. He still had the ability to hold people's attention, and he attracted large audiences. For Jefferson, it was a happy time. His homeland and its people still loved and respected him.

Jefferson kept up his busy lecture schedule until the winter of 1889, when he fell very ill. On December 6, 1889, he died at the age of 81. Southerners did not forget him. They memorialized him with a huge funeral procession, which surprised many Northerners. They mistakenly believed he was not respected in the South.

Jefferson was buried in New Orleans. Later, Varina moved his remains to Richmond. A monument to his memory now stands in the old Confederate capital. An inscription reads, "Jefferson Davis, the first and only President of the Confederate States of America."

Jefferson Davis had lived a long life, some of it filled with happiness, much of it filled with struggle. Often at the expense of his own health, he worked tirelessly for the Confederacy. Jefferson

Southerners remember Jefferson's leadership in this monument in Richmond, Virginia.

was a courageous soldier and a brave leader who stood firm for what he believed in. Although he wanted to keep the United States one nation, he nevertheless willingly took responsibility and served the South when its people called on him.

GLOSSARY

abolitionist–a person who wanted to abolish, or do away with, slavery

aggression–a warlike act of a person or nation against another

bankrupt–having no money or other means to pay one's debts

civil war–a war between people who live in the same nation

Confederate States of America–the name of the nation formed by the 11 Southern states that left the United States

convert–to change from one idea or belief to another

discipline–training by control or punishment

Emancipation Proclamation–the order by President Abraham Lincoln that freed the slaves in the South

frontier–a place where settled land meets a wilderness

inaugurate–to place a person, such as a president, in an office with a special ceremony

invade–to enter a place or land as an enemy

legislature–a part of government organized to make laws

militia–citizens who volunteer to keep order in times of trouble

plantation–an estate or large farm that produces a major crop

secede–to leave a group or a nation

siege–a military effort to capture a place by surrounding it

skirmish–a small battle

slave–a person who is the property of another and can be bought and sold

squatters–people who live on a property without permission

strategy–the planning and directing of something, such as military operations

thoroughbred–a breed of light, speedy horses

treaty–an agreement, especially among nations, that each approves

Union–states that remained part of the United States in the Civil War

CHRONOLOGY

1808   Born Jefferson Finis Davis on June 3 in Christian County (now Todd County), Kentucky.

1811–12 Family moves to Louisiana and then to Mississippi.

1824   Enters United States Military Academy at West Point, New York.

1828   Graduates from West Point and joins the army.

1835   Resigns from the army and becomes a cotton planter; marries Sarah Knox Taylor on June 17; Sarah dies of malaria on September 15.

1843   Runs for Mississippi legislature.

1845   Marries Varina Howell; elected to the House of Representatives.

1846–47 Rejoins the army as colonel; becomes a hero at Battle of Buena Vista during the Mexican War; is appointed senator representing Mississippi.

1851   Resigns from Senate and runs for governor of Mississippi.

1852   Serves as secretary of war under President Franklin Pierce.

1861   Announces secession of Mississippi and delivers farewell address to U.S. Senate.

1862   Inaugurated as president of the Confederate States of America and leads the Confederacy during the Civil War.

1865	Flees from Richmond, Virginia; is captured by Union forces at Irwinville, Georgia.
1867–78	Released from prison; travels in Europe; lives in various places in the South; fails in business; tours the South giving lectures; retires to New Orleans, Louisiana.
1881	Completes his book, *The Rise and Fall of the Confederate Government.*
1889	Dies on December 6 at his home in New Orleans.

CIVIL WAR TIME LINE

1860   Abraham Lincoln is elected president of the United States on November 6. During the next few months, Southern states begin to break away from the Union.

1861   On April 12, the Confederates attack Fort Sumter, South Carolina, and the Civil War begins. Union forces are defeated in Virginia at the First Battle of Bull Run (First Manassas) on July 21 and withdraw to Washington, D.C.

1862   Robert E. Lee is placed in command of the main Confederate army in Virginia in June. Lee defeats the Army of the Potomac at the Second Battle of Bull Run (Second Manassas) in Virginia on August 29–30. On September 17, Union general George B. McClellan turns back Lee's first invasion of the North at Antietam Creek near Sharpsburg, Maryland. It is the bloodiest day of the war.

1863   On January 1, President Lincoln issues the Emancipation Proclamation, freeing slaves in Southern states. Between May 1–6, Lee wins an important victory at Chancellorsville, but key Southern commander Thomas J. "Stonewall" Jackson dies from wounds. In June, Union forces hold the city of Vicksburg, Mississippi, under siege. The people of Vicksburg surrender on July 4. Lee's second invasion of the North during July 1–3 is decisively turned back at Gettysburg, Pennsylvania.

1864   General Grant is made supreme Union commander on March 9. Following a series of costly battles, on June 19 Grant successfully encircles Lee's troops in Petersburg, Virginia. A siege of the town lasts nearly a year. Union general William Sherman captures Atlanta on September 2 and begins the "March to the Sea," a campaign of destruction across Georgia and South Carolina. On November 8, Abraham Lincoln wins reelection as president.

1865   On April 2, Petersburg, Virginia, falls to the Union. Lee attempts to reach Confederate forces in North Carolina but is gradually surrounded by Union troops. Lee surrenders to Grant on April 9 at Appomattox, Virginia, ending the war. Abraham Lincoln is assassinated by John Wilkes Booth on April 14.

FURTHER READING

Golay, Michael. *The Civil War*. New York: Facts on File, 1992.

Green, Carl R., and William R. Sanford. *Confederate Generals of the Civil War*. Springfield, N.J.: Enslow Publishers, 1998.

Kent, Zachary. *The Story of the Surrender at Appomattox Court House*. Chicago: Children's Press, 1987.

Marrin, Albert. *Unconditional Surrender: U.S. Grant and the Civil War*. New York: Atheneum, 1994.

Murphy, Jim. *The Boys' War*. New York: Clarion Books, 1990.

INDEX

PICKURE CREDITS ══════════════

page

3: The Library of Congress
6: New Millennium Images
11: The Library of Congress
16: West Point Library/
    U.S. Military Academy
18: New Millennium Images
23: New Millennium Images
28: New York Public Library/
    Picture Collections
31: New Millennium Images
36: The Library of Congress
41: The Library of Congress

43: The Library of Congress
46: New York Public Library/
    Picture Collections
48: The Library of Congress
54: The Library of Congress
59: The Library of Congress
60: New Millennium Images
62: New York Public Library/
    Picture Collections
67: New Millennium Images
70: New Millennium Images

ABOUT THE AUTHOR

JOEY FRAZIER is a freelance writer and editor in Lexington, South Carolina, who enjoys military history and collecting artifacts. He has a degree in English from the University of South Carolina.

Senior Consulting Editor **ARTHUR M. SCHLESINGER, JR.** is the leading American historian of our time. He won the Pulitzer Prize for his book *The Age of Jackson* (1945), and again for *A Thousand Days* (1965). This chronicle of the Kennedy Administration also won a National Book Award. He has written many other books, including a multi-volume series, *The Age of Roosevelt.* Professor Schlesinger is the Albert Schweitzer Professor of the Humanities at the City University of New York, and has been involved in several other Chelsea House projects, including the COLONIAL LEADERS series of biographies on the most prominent figures of early American history.